GIFTED
GAMES™

GIFTED AND TALENTED
COGAT® TEST PREP

for children in preschool and kindergarten

Gateway Gifted Resources™
www.GatewayGifted.com

PLEASE LEAVE US A REVIEW!

Thank you for selecting this book. We are a family-owned publishing company - a consortium of educators, book designers, illustrators, parents, and kid-testers.

We would be thrilled if you left us a quick review on the website where you purchased this book!

The Gateway Gifted Resources™ Team
www.GatewayGifted.com

TABLE OF CONTENTS

INTRODUCTION

ABOUT THIS BOOK

This book introduces reasoning exercises, problem-solving tasks, and cognitive skill-building activities to young children through kid-friendly subjects, all in a format designed to help prepare them for taking standardized multiple-choice gifted and talented assessment tests.

Not only is this book meant to help prepare children for the COGAT®, these critical thinking and logic-based materials may also be used as general academic support as well as for other gifted test prep.

THIS BOOK HAS 5 PARTS:

1. Introduction (p. 4-9)
- About This Book
- About Gifted Tests
- Test-Taking Tips
- The "Gifted Detective Agency"

2. Gifted Workbook (p. 10-48)
- Pages 10-21 are designed as skill-building activities, while pages 22-48 are designed similarly to content tested in the COGAT®'s nine test sections. (See pages 6-7 for more on these sections.)
- This workbook offers fun, kid-friendly themes to engage children and introduce them to standardized gifted test formats.
- The exercises are meant to be done together with no time limit.
- Some sections include additional explanations and tips. Be sure to read these.

The "Gifted Detective Agency"
To increase child engagement and to add an incentive to complete book exercises, a detective theme accompanies this book. Read page 9 ("Gifted Detective Agency") together with your child. The book's characters belong to a detective agency. They want your child to help them solve "puzzles" (the exercises in the book) so that your child can join the detective agency, too! As your child completes the book, allow him/her to "check" the boxes at the bottom of the page. If your child "checks all the boxes," (s)he will "join" the Gifted Detective Agency. We have included boxes at the bottom of every page of the book that features exercises. However, feel free to modify as you see fit the number of pages/exercises your child must complete in order to receive his/her certificate.

(The certificate for you to complete with your child's name is on page 96.)

3. Practice Question Set (p. 50-90)

The Practice Question Set provides:
- an introduction for children to test-taking in a relaxed manner, where parents can provide guidance if needed (without telling the answers!)
- an opportunity for children to practice focusing on a group of questions for a longer time period (something to which most children are not accustomed)

  a way for parents to identify points of strength and weakness in various types of test questions

The Practice Question Set is meant to help children develop critical thinking and test-taking skills. A "score" (a percentile rank) cannot be obtained from the Practice Question Set. (See page 6 for more on gifted test scoring.)

4. Directions and Answer Keys (p. 91-95)

(Please use a pair of scissors to cut out pages 91-95.) These pages provide answer keys for both the Workbook and the Practice Question Set. They also include the directions to read to your child for the Practice Question Set. (To mimic actual tests, the directions are separate from the child's pages in the Practice Question Set.)

5. Afterword (p.96)

Information on additional books, free 40+ practice questions, and your child's certificate

A NOTE ON FILLING IN "BUBBLES"

Your child may or may not have to fill in "bubbles" (the circles) to indicate answer choices. When taking a standardized gifted test, if your child is at the Pre-K level, (s)he will most likely only have to point to the answer choice. If your child is at the Kindergarten level, (s)he may have to fill in bubbles. Check with your testing site regarding its "bubble" use.

If your child is at the Kindergarten level, show him/her the "bubbles" under the answer choices. Show your child how to fill in the bubble to indicate his/her answer choice. If your child needs to change his/her answer, (s)he should erase the original mark and fill in the new choice.

A NOTE ON THE QUESTIONS

Because each child has different cognitive abilities, the questions in this book are at varied skill levels. The exercises may or may not require a great deal of parental guidance to complete, depending on your child's ability.

You will notice that most sections of the Workbook begin with a relatively easy question. We suggest always completing at least the first question (which will most likely be an easy one) with him/her. Make sure there is not any confusion about what the question asks or with the directions.

WHAT YOU NEED

- *Gifted Games* book
- Answer Keys/Directions (pages 91-95) cut out and by your side
- Pencil and eraser for your child

ABOUT GIFTED TESTS

Gifted tests, like the COGAT®, assess a child's cognitive abilities, reasoning skills, and problem-solving aptitude.

Testing procedures vary by school and/or program. These tests may be given individually or in a group environment, by a teacher or other testing examiner. These tests may be used as the single determinant for admission to a selective kindergarten or to a school's gifted program. However, some schools/programs use these tests in combination with individual IQ tests administered by psychologists or as part of a student "portfolio." Other schools use them together with tests like Iowa Assessments™ to measure academic achievement. In other instances, schools/programs may use only certain sections of the tests to screen. (See below for more information on test sections.) **Check with your testing site to determine its specific testing procedures.**

Here is a general summary of the scoring process for multiple-choice standardized gifted tests. **Please check with your school/program for its specific scoring and admissions requirements.** First, your child's raw score is established. The raw score equals the number of questions your daughter/son correctly answered. Points are not deducted for questions answered incorrectly. Next, this score is compared to other test-takers of his/her same age group (and, for the COGAT®, the same grade level) using various indices to then calculate your child's stanine (a score from one to nine) and percentile rank. If your child achieved the percentile rank of 98%, then (s)he scored as well as or better than 98% of test-takers. In general, most gifted programs only accept top performers of *at least* 98% or *higher*.

(Please note that a percentile rank "score" cannot be obtained from our practice material. This material has not been given to a large enough sample of test-takers to develop any kind of base score necessary for percentile rank calculations.)

COGAT® (COGNITIVE ABILITIES TEST®) LEVEL 5/6

The COGAT® Level 5/6 is given to children in Kindergarten. It has 118 questions. The test, about two-hours in length, is administered in different testing sessions. (Children are not expected to complete 118 questions in one session.) Check with your school regarding which level your child will take and for specific test procedures.

The COGAT® measures reasoning skills through exercises including: object classification, identification of similarities/differences, recognizing relationships, analogy completion, sequence completion, pattern completion, quantitative concepts and basic math activities, spatial concept comprehension, and basic vocabulary comprehension.

The COGAT® consists of three sections (each called a "Battery": the Verbal Battery, Quantitative Battery, and Non-Verbal Battery) and contains the nine question types below.

Verbal Battery

Picture Analogies

Picture Classification

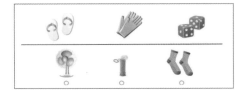

Sentence Completion

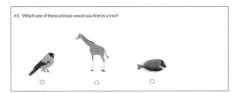

Quantitative Battery

Number Series

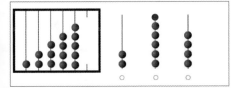

Number Puzzles

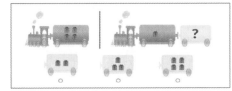

Number Analogies

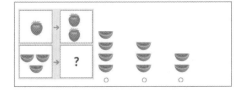

Non-Verbal Battery

Figure Analogies

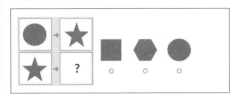

Figure Classification

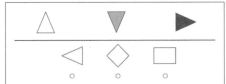

Paper Folding

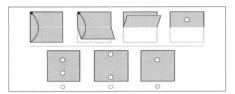

Pages 22-48 of the Workbook, as well as the COGAT® Practice Question Set (pages 50-90), are organized by question type. We suggest referencing question type labels listed at the top of pages 22-48 of the Workbook, and listed on pages 91-95 in the Practice Question Set Answer Key, in order to gain a better understanding of the material in each question type. After your child completes the Practice Question Set, you can use the Answer Key to evaluate your child's strengths/weaknesses by question type.

TEST-TAKING TIPS

Listening Skills: Have your child practice listening carefully to questions and following the directions in this book. Paying attention is important, because often test questions are not repeated by the test administrator.

Work Through The Exercise: In the Workbook section of this book, go through the exercises together by talking about them: what the exercise is asking the child to do and what makes the answer choices correct/incorrect. This will not only familiarize your child with working through exercises, it will also help him/her develop a process of elimination (getting rid of any answer choices that are incorrect).

Answer Choices: Make sure your child looks at **each** answer choice. You may wish to point to each answer choice if you notice your child not looking at each one.

Guessing: For the test outlined in this book, test-takers receive points for the number of correct answers. It is advantageous to at least guess instead of leaving a question unanswered. If your child says that (s)he does not know the answer, (s)he should first eliminate any answers that are obviously not correct. Then, (s)he can guess from those remaining.

Choose ONE Answer: Remind your child to choose only ONE answer. If your child has a test with "answer bubbles," remind him/her that he/she must fill in only ONE bubble per question. If your child must instead point to an answer, remind him/her to point to only one answer per question.

Negative Words: In the Sentence Completion section, (s)he should listen carefully for "negative words" ("no", "not", "nor", "neither") and negative prefixes like "un-".

Common Sense Tips: Children are like adults when it comes to common sense exam-readiness for test day. Make sure your child:

- is familiar with the test site (If the exam will be at a location that is new to your child, go to the testing site together before test day. Simply driving by or walking by the outside of the building not only ensures you know how to reach the site; it also will give your child a sense of familiarity, come test day.)
- is well-rested
- has eaten a breakfast for sustained energy and concentration (complex carbohydrates and protein; avoid foods/drinks high in sugar)
- has a chance to use the restroom prior to the test (The administrator may not allow a break during the test.)

Try not to get overly-stressed about the gifted testing process (as difficult as that may be). It is surprising how much children can sense from adults, and children learn best through play. So, the more fun that you can make test prep (by using something like a detective theme!), the better.

THE GIFTED DETECTIVE AGENCY *(Read this page with your child.)*

Alex

May

Sophie

Anya

Freddie

Max

We're the Gifted Detective Agency. We need another member, someone else to join us. We think YOU have what it takes!

"What does a detective do?" you may ask. Well, a detective figures out puzzles, solves problems, and finds answers to questions.

To prove you're ready to join the Gifted Detective Agency, you'll put your skills to the test in this book. Together with your mom, dad, or other adult, you need to solve puzzles. The adult helping you will explain what to do, so listen carefully!

A good detective:
- Pays attention and listens closely
- Looks carefully at all choices before answering a question
- Keeps trying even if some questions are hard

After you finish the questions on each page, mark the box at the bottom. Like this:

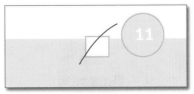

Your parent (or other adult) will tell you which pages to do. After finishing them all, you will become a member of the Gifted Detective Agency! (Remember, it's more important to answer the questions the right way than to try to finish them really fast.) After you're done, you'll get your very own Gifted Detective Agency certificate.

When you're ready to start the puzzles, write your name here: _____

SOPHIE NEEDS YOUR HELP TO ANSWER THESE QUESTIONS!

Directions: Look at the items in the box. They are related in some way and belong together. Think about how they belong together.

Next, look at the items under the box. Let's figure out which of these would belong with the items in the box. Some would belong and some would not. Draw a circle around the things that would belong. Draw an "X" on the things that would not belong.

1.

SOPHIE NEEDS YOUR HELP AGAIN, THIS TIME WITH SHAPES!

2.

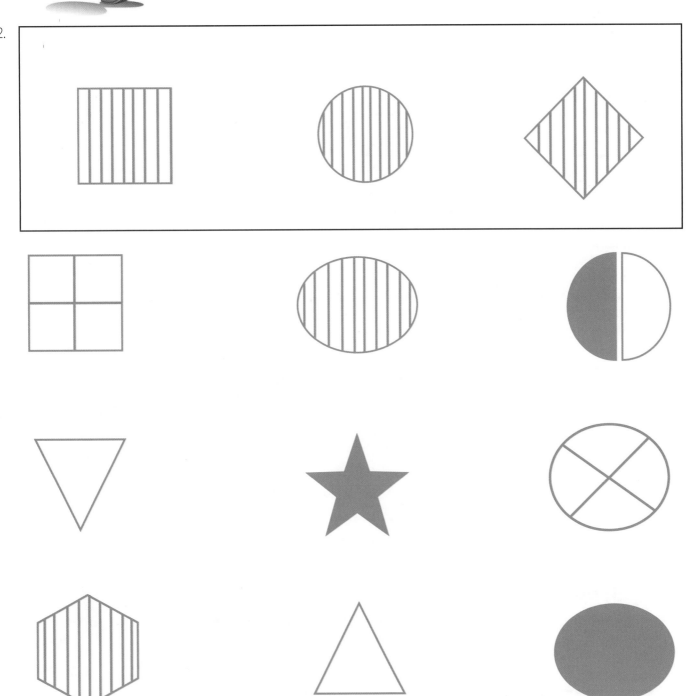

WILL YOU HELP ANYA FIND THE PICTURES THAT ARE EXACTLY THE SAME?

Directions: Look at the picture in the first box. Then, look at the group of pictures in the next box. Find the picture or pictures that are exactly the same as the picture in the first box. There could be more than one picture that is exactly the same, so look carefully.

1.

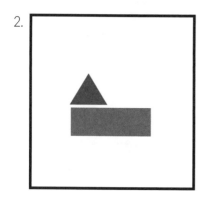 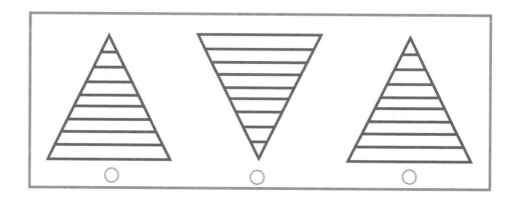

2.

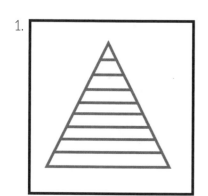 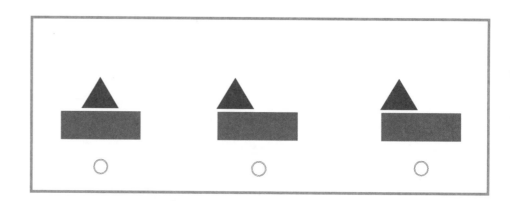

3.

4.

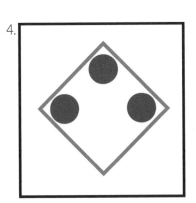
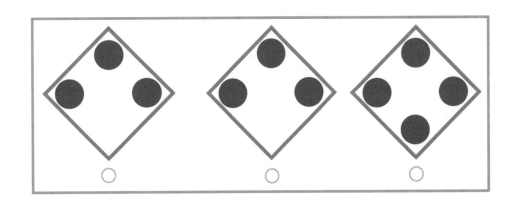

5.

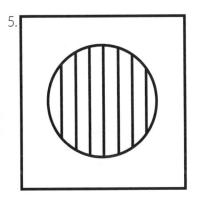
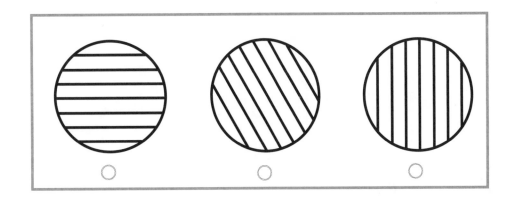

6.

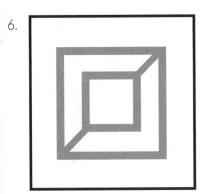
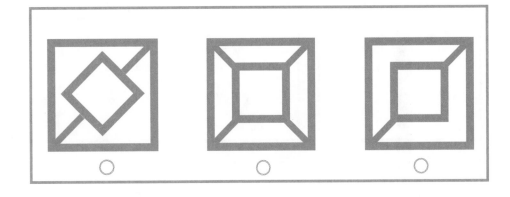

7.

WILL YOU HELP MAX ANSWER THESE QUESTIONS?

Directions: Look at the picture in the first box. Then, look at the group of pictures in the next box. Which picture from the group would go the best with the picture that is in the first box?

1.
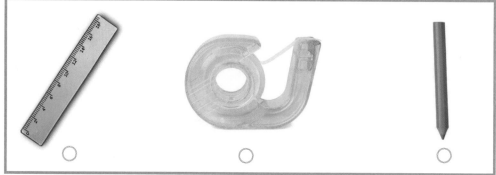

2.
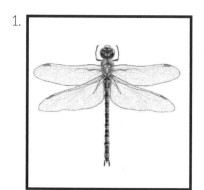

3.

NOW, LET'S DO THE SAME THING WITH SHAPES!

1.

2.

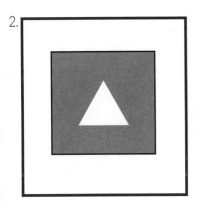 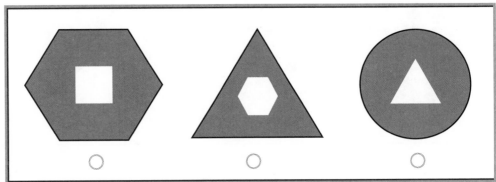

3.

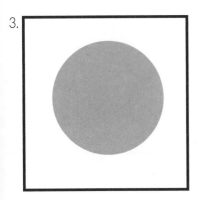 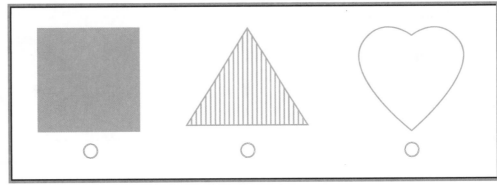

4.

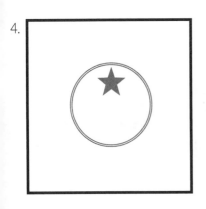 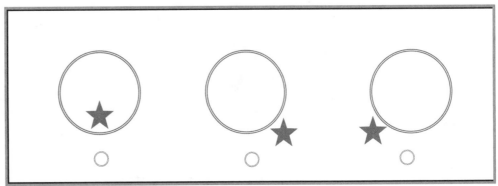

FREDDIE NEEDS YOUR HELP TO FIGURE OUT WHICH PICTURE DOESN'T BELONG!

Directions: Look at this row of pictures. One of these pictures in the row does not belong. This picture is not like the others in the row. Which picture does not belong?

1.

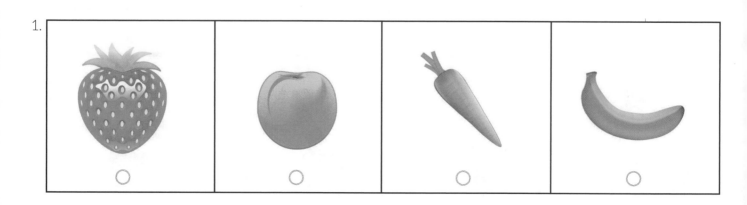

2.

3.

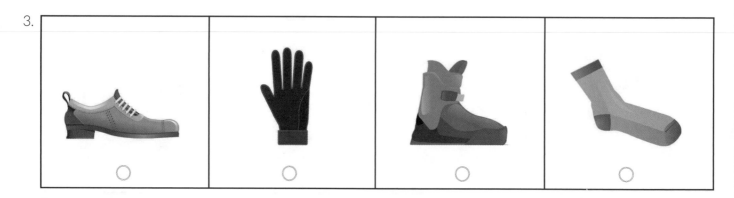

4.

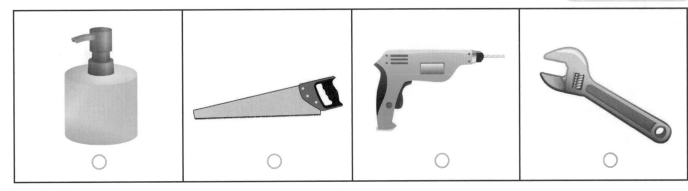

5.

6.

7.

8.

9.

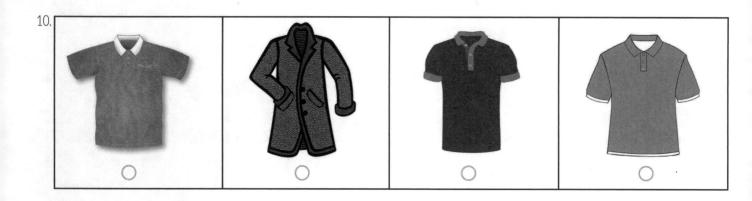

10.

11.

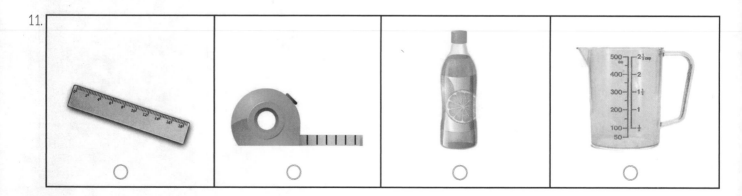

12.

13.

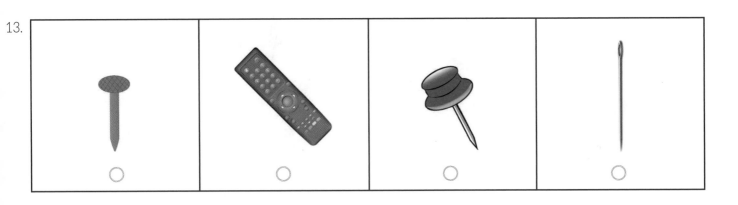

YOU'RE DOING GREAT!

FREDDIE SAYS, "YOU'RE DOING GREAT!" NOW, LET'S DO THE SAME THING WITH SHAPES.

1.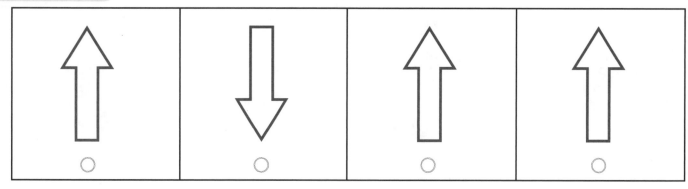

2.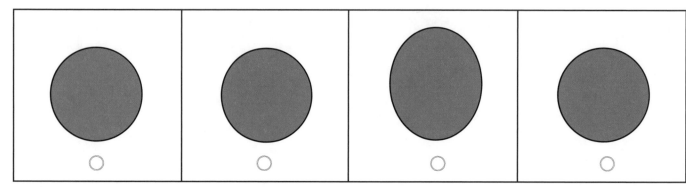

3.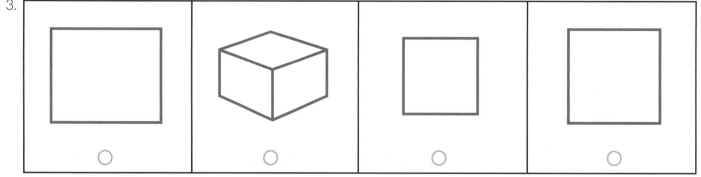

4.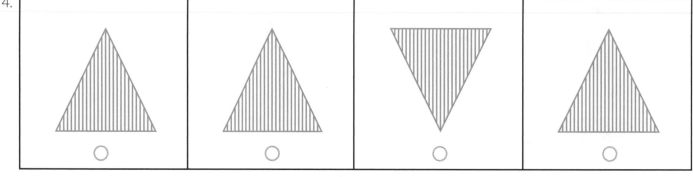

5.

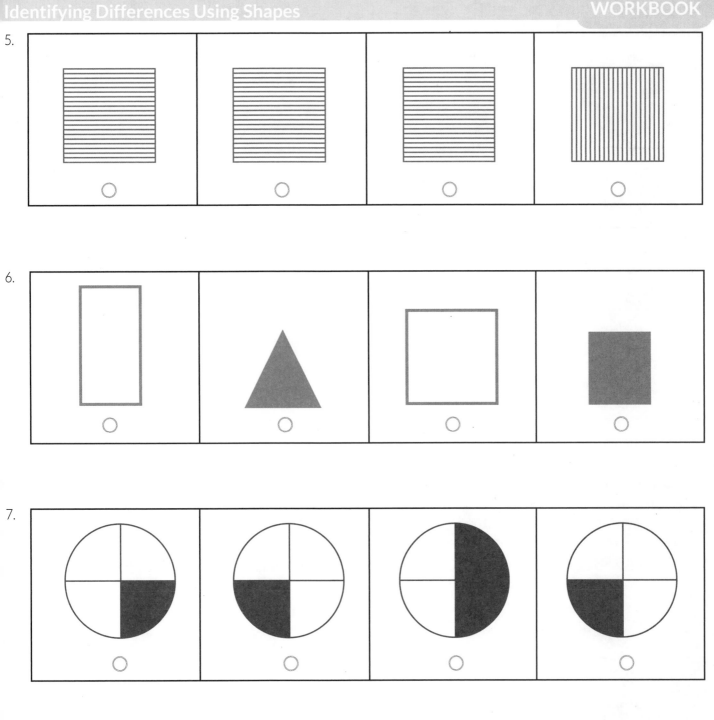

6.

7.

8.

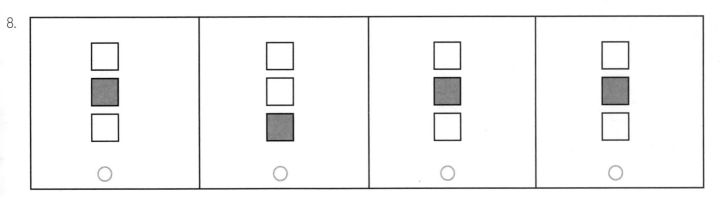

HELP ALEX FIND OUT WHAT GOES IN THE EMPTY BOX!

Directions: Look at these boxes that are on top. The pictures that are inside belong together in some way. Then, look at these boxes that are on the bottom. One of these boxes on the bottom is empty. Look next to the boxes. There is a row of pictures. Which one would go together with this picture that is in the bottom box like these pictures that are in the top boxes?

Parent note: Analogies are a new kind of "puzzle" for most young kids. They compare sets of items, and the way they are related can easily be missed at first. Work through these together with your child so (s)he sees how the top set is related. Together, try to come up with a "rule" to describe how the top set is related. Then, look at the picture on the bottom. Take this "rule," use it together with the picture on the bottom, and figure out which of the answer choices would follow that same rule. (The small arrows show that the pictures belong together in some way.)

Everyday life presents a great opportunity for skill-building, as common themes for Picture Analogies and Picture Classification (p.28) include: the function and uses of common items, clothing, animals (types of animals, their homes, habitats, and development), transportation, food, professions/ community helpers, musical instruments, parts of the body, sports, and object characteristics (color, shape, quantity, size, position).

Example (read this to your child): Look at the boxes on top. There are two umbrellas. (Talk about the two pictures and try to come up with a "rule.") The item in the first box is open. The item in the next box is closed. What is in the bottom box? It is a book, and the book is open. Now, let's look at the answer choices. Which one goes with the picture of the open book in the same way that the pictures in the top row go together? A closed book. In the top boxes, first the umbrella is open, and then it closes. In the bottom box, the book is open, so the correct answer choice is a closed book.

1.

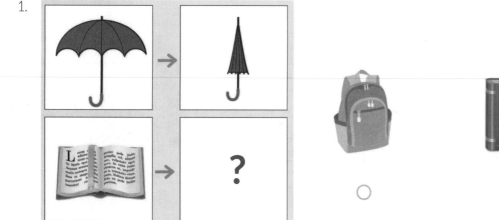

2.

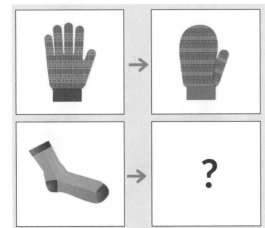

○   ○   ○

3.

○   ○   ○

4.

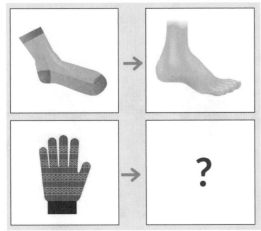

○   ○   ○

5.

→

?

○

○

○

6.

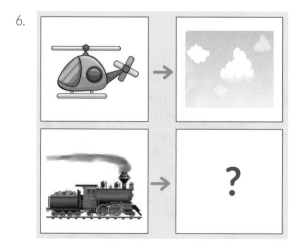

?

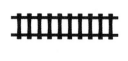
○

○

○

7.

?

○

○

○

8.

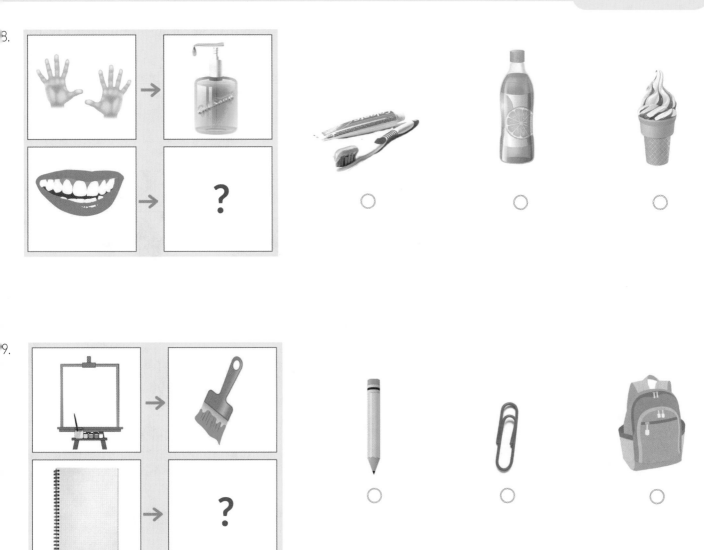

9.

LET'S HELP ALEX ANSWER THE SAME KIND OF QUESTION ON THE NEXT PAGE, BUT NOW WE'LL USE SHAPES!

Parent Note: As you did with Picture Analogies, together, come up with a "rule" to describe how the top set is related. With Figure Analogies, often this rule will describe how the picture in the left box "changes" into the picture in the right box. Common "changes" include shape type (i.e., #1), shape color (i.e., #2, #3, #6), whole and half (i.e., #4), size (i.e.,#5), direction shape is pointing (i.e., #80 in Practice Test), shape quantity (i.e., #81 in Practice Test), and shape "flipping" to appear as a mirror image of original (#82, #84 in Practice Test).

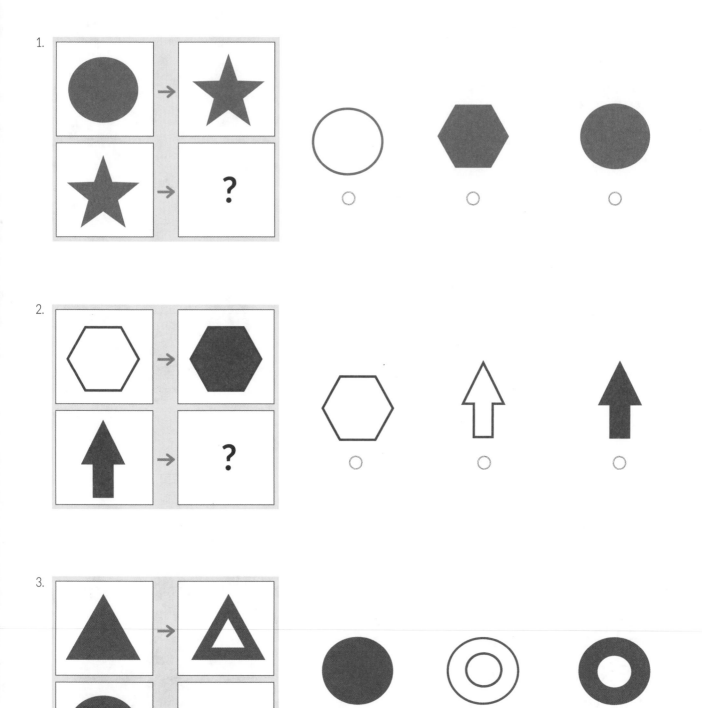

1.

2.

3.

4.

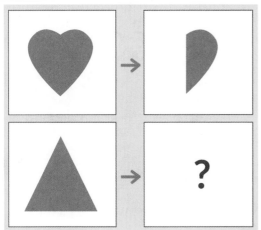

○   ○   ○

5.

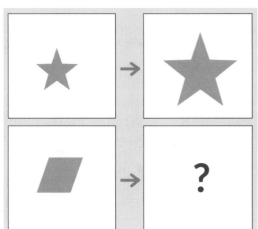

○   ○   ○

6.

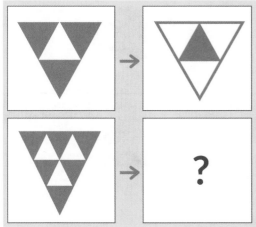

○   ○   ○

WILL YOU HELP MAY FIGURE OUT THESE PUZZLES?

Directions: Look at the top row of pictures. These pictures are alike in a certain way.

Then, look at the pictures that are on the bottom row.

Which picture that is in the bottom row would go best with the pictures that are in the top row?

Example (read this to your child): Let's look at the top row of pictures. We see a cupcake, a lollipop, and chocolate. Let's think about how these are alike. Let's come up with a "rule" to describe how they each are alike.

You can eat each of these, and they are sweets.

Let's look at the bottom row. We need to find the answer choice on the bottom that follows the same rule. We see ice cream, a drink, and a piece of pizza.

Which one of these goes best with the pictures of the sweets in the top row? Ice cream! You can eat ice cream, and it is a sweet.

1.

○   ○   ○

2.

3.

4.

5.

○   ○   ○

6.

○   ○   ○

7.

○   ○   ○

8.

○ ○ ○

9.

○ ○ ○

LET'S HELP MAY ANSWER THE SAME KIND OF QUESTION ON THE NEXT PAGE, BUT NOW WE'LL USE SHAPES!

1.

○ ○ ○

2.

○ ○ ○

3.

○ ○ ○

4.

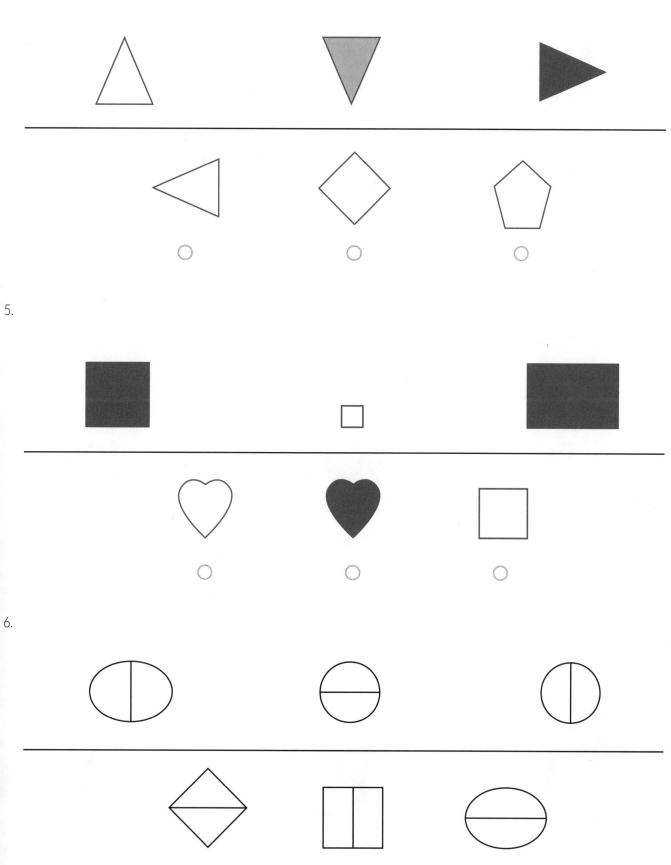

5.

6.

LET'S HELP ANYA AND MAX ANSWER THESE QUESTIONS.

Directions: Listen to the question and then choose your answer.

Parent Note: These exercises are similar to those on the Sentence Completion section of the COGAT®. Try to read each question only one time to your child so that (s)he can practice listening skills.

1. Which one of these would you see at a playground?

2. Which of these would you wear when it is hot outside?

3. Which of these would you wear when it is cold outside?

○

4. Which of these is a pair?

○

○

○

5. Which one of these animals would you find in a tree?

○

○

○

LET'S GIVE ALEX A HAND!

Directions: Look at the top row of pictures. These show a sheet of paper and how it was folded. Look at these pictures that are on the bottom row. Which picture shows how the paper would look after the paper is unfolded?

Parent note: The paper folding exercises may be difficult at first for your child. If so, go through the exercises together using a real sheet of paper.

1.

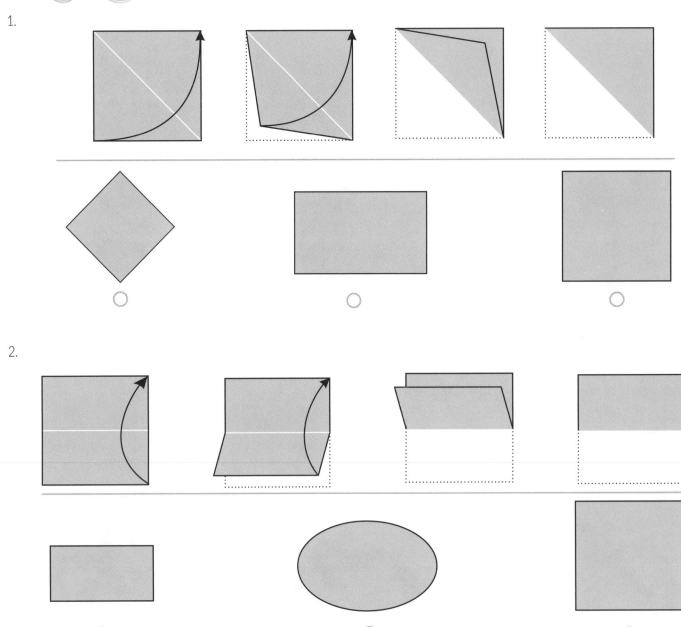

2.

YOU'RE GOING TO BE A GREAT DETECTIVE!

Directions: Look at the top row of pictures. These show a sheet of paper, how it was folded, and how holes were made in the folded sheet of paper. Look at these pictures that are on the bottom row. Which picture shows how the paper would look after the paper is unfolded?

Parent note: To help your child better understand these exercises, demonstrate using real paper and a hole puncher (or scissors). Be sure to point out the placement of the holes and the number of holes you make in the paper.

3.

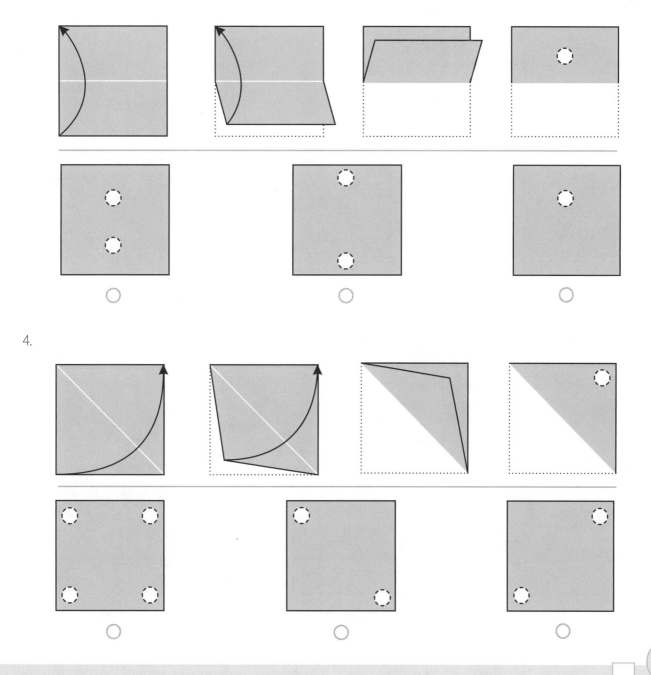

4.

NICE WORK, LET'S DO SOME MORE.

Directions: Look at the top row of pictures. These show a sheet of paper, how it was folded, and how holes were made in the folded sheet of paper. Look at these pictures that are on the bottom row. Which picture shows how the paper would look after the paper is unfolded?

5.

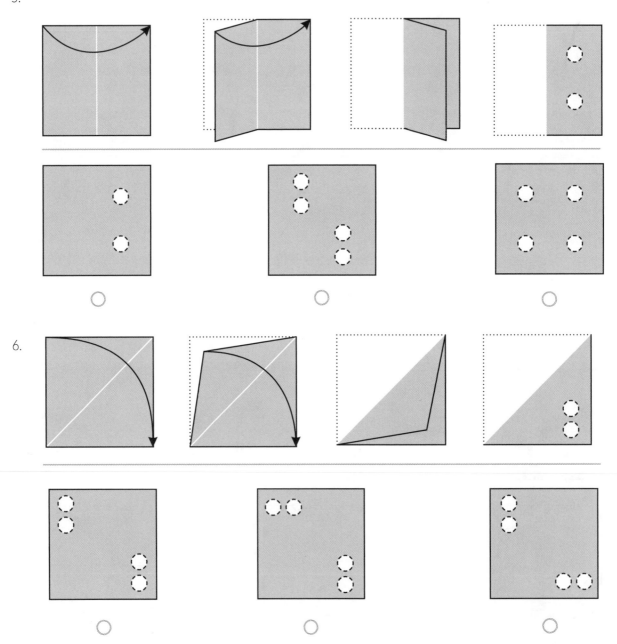

6.

LET'S HELP ALEX WITH A FEW OTHERS!

Directions: Look at the top row of pictures. These show a sheet of paper and how it was folded. The picture with the scissors shows where a part of the folded sheet of paper was cut out. On the bottom row, which picture shows how the sheet of paper would look after the paper is unfolded?

Parent note: To help your child better understand these exercises, demonstrate using real paper and scissors. Be sure to point out the placement of the part that is cut out.

7.

 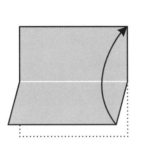  

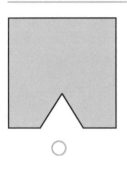 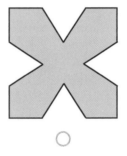 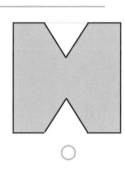

○ ○ ○

8.

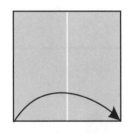 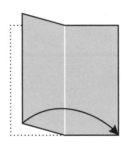  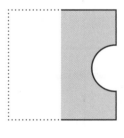

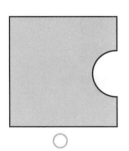 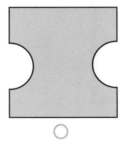 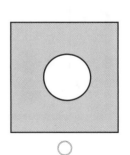

○ ○ ○

LET'S GIVE FREDDIE A HAND WITH SOME NUMBER PUZZLES.

Section explanation: An abacus is a toy with rods and beads that is used for counting. Here, the final rod of the abacus is missing. The first five rods of the abacus have a pattern. Have your child look closely at these five to determine the pattern. The last rod is missing. (S)he will then need to select which rod would finish the pattern. Make sure your child carefully and correctly counts the number of abacus beads. Note that some answer choices do not have any beads. This equals "0". Due to the complexity of this question type, we have included detailed directions for the first question.

Directions for first question: Here's an abacus. The "circles" on the abacus are beads. These beads are on rods. The beads in the first five rods have made a pattern. Look at the last rod on the abacus. The beads on this rod are missing.

Next to the abacus are three rods. These are the answer choices. Choose which rod would go in the place of the last rod in order to complete the pattern.

Let's look at the abacus. We see 1 bead, then 2 beads, then 3 beads, then 4 beads, then 5 beads. Do you see a pattern? On each rod, one bead gets added. What would go after the rod with 5 beads? If one bead gets added each time, what would go after 5 beads? The last rod on the abacus is missing. What rod goes here to finish the pattern? (Look at each answer choice.) It is the rod with 6 beads.

Directions for the rest: Which rod would go in the place of the missing rod to finish the pattern?

1.

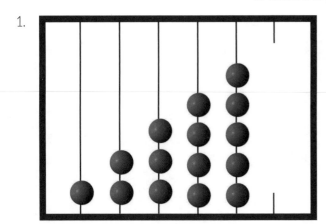

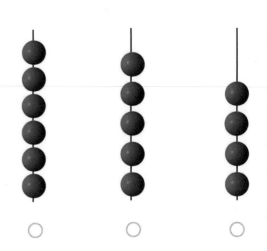

2.

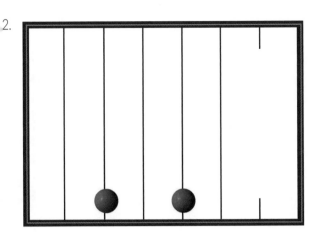 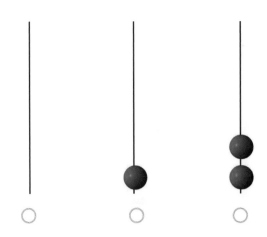

3.

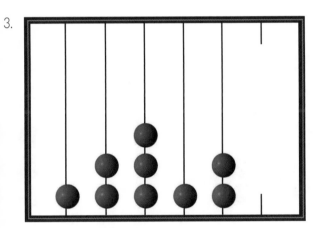 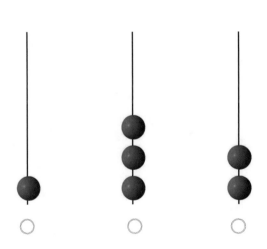

4.

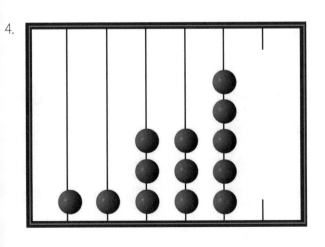 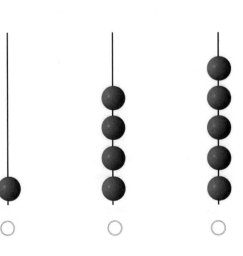

5.

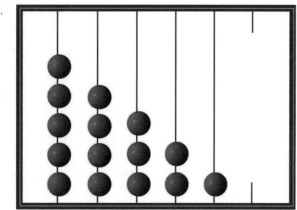

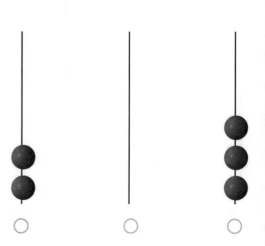

6.

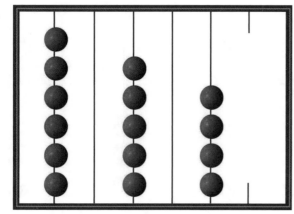

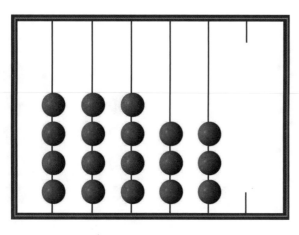

7.

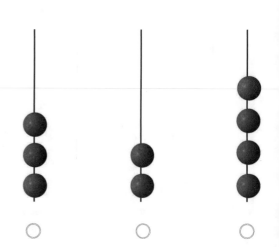

MAX NEEDS YOUR HELP WITH THESE NUMBER GAMES!

Section explanation: Here are two trains, one on the top and one on the bottom. Each train must have the same total number of things. Your child needs to figure out which answer choice would go in place of the car(s) with the question mark. The train on the top must have the same total number of things as the one on the bottom. Make sure your child carefully and correctly counts the number of things (presents or fruit, in these questions). Due to the complexity of this question type, we have included detailed directions for the first question.

Directions for first question: Look at the first train, the one on the top. It has 4 presents.

Look at the train on the bottom, the second train. This train has 1 present. You need to put a train car in place of the train car that has a question mark so that the second train has the same number of presents as the other train.

Which train car should you choose so that the second train has 4 presents all together? It would be the train car that has 3 presents. One plus three equals four. Now the two trains would have the same number.

Directions for the rest: Which train car should you choose so that the second train has the same number of things as the first?

1.

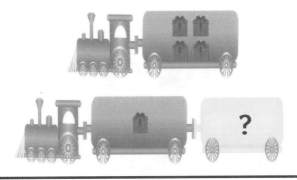

○   ○   ○

2.

◯   ◯   ◯

3.

   ◯   ◯

◯   ◯   ◯

4.

◯   ◯   ◯

5.

 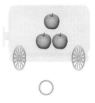

○　　　　　　　○　　　　　　　○

6.

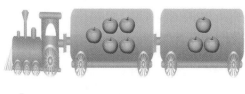

○　　　　　　　○　　　　　　　○

7.

○　　　　　　　○　　　　　　　○

SOPHIE NEEDS A HAND WITH NUMBER GAMES!

Section explanation: Number analogies questions are similar to the other analogy questions earlier in this book. Here, however, the top set of boxes and the bottom set of boxes must have the same type of quantitative relationship. Your child must figure out which one of the answer choices would go in the empty box with the question mark to complete the mathematical analogy. Due to the complexity of this section, we have included detailed directions for the first question.

Directions for first question: The top boxes belong together in some way. Look at the top box on the left - there is one strawberry. Look at the top box on the right - there are two strawberries. What has changed between the picture on the left and the picture on the right? We need to come up with a "rule" to describe what has happened. The right box has one more strawberry than the left box. One strawberry was added to get the number of strawberries in the right box.

Next, let's look carefully at the boxes in the bottom row. The first box has three pieces of watermelon. The second box is empty. Look carefully at the row of pictures next to the boxes. Which one of these goes in the empty box? The answer is "four pieces of watermelon." On the bottom row, the first box has three pieces of watermelon. If you add one more, then you have four pieces of watermelon.

Directions for the rest: Which answer choice would go inside the empty box at the bottom?

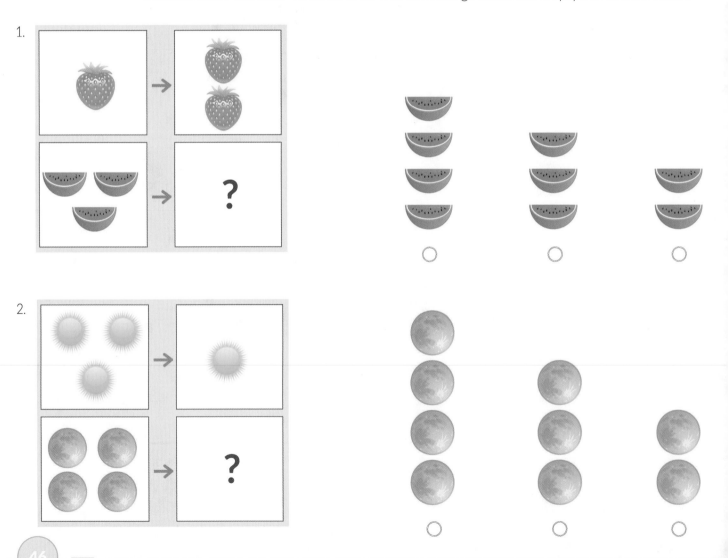

3.

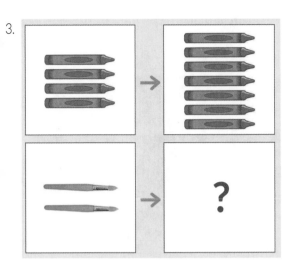

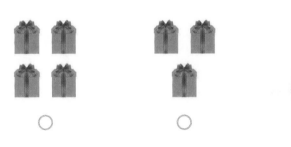

4.

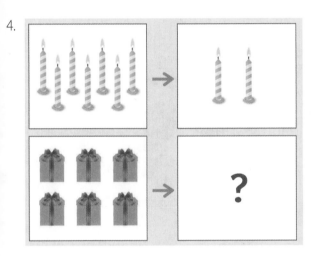

5.

6.

7.

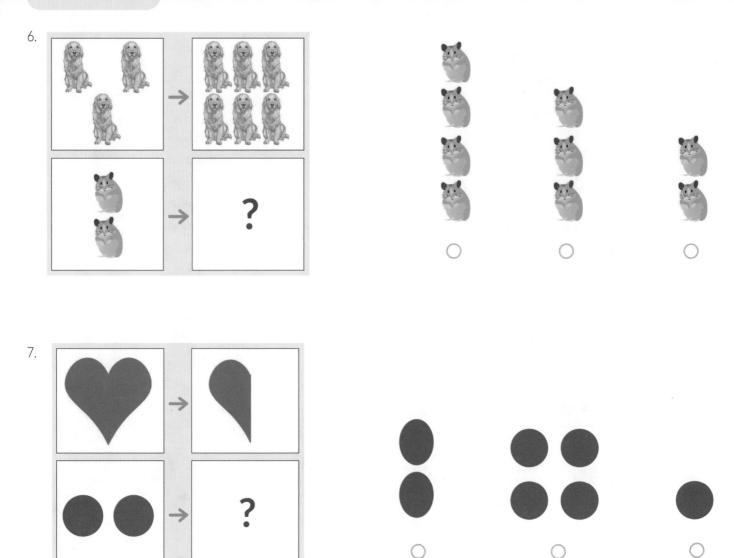

This is the end of the Workbook section. The Practice Question Set exercises begin on page 50.

PRACTICE QUESTION SET INSTRUCTIONS

✂ Please cut out pages 91-95. Page 91 is the Workbook Answer Key. Pages 91-95 are the Directions and Answer Key for the Practice Question Set. These include question prompts.

Reading Directions: Tell your child to listen carefully (like a detective!), because you can read the directions to him/her only one time. (Test administrators often read directions only once.)

Test instructors will not let your child know if his/her answers are correct/incorrect. If you wish for the Practice Question Set to serve as a "practice test," then as your child completes the Practice Question Set, we suggest you do the same. Instead of saying if answers are correct/incorrect, you could say something like, "Nice work, let's try some more."

Navigation Figures: Assuming your child has completed the Workbook, then (s)he is familiar with the exercise format (navigating through pages with rows of questions). To make the test navigation easier for kids, some gifted tests use image markers in place of question numbers and in place of page numbers.

We include the "markers" so that your child can be familiar with them.

When your child needs to look at a new page, you would say, for example, "Find the page where there is an umbrella at the bottom." When your child needs to look at a question, you would say, for example, "Find the row where there is a bug." The markers are listed on the Directions & Answer Key pages so that you can read them to your child.

"Bubbles" and Answer Choices: If your child is at the Kindergarten level, (s)he may have to fill in "bubbles" (the circles) to indicate answer choice. The Practice Question Set has answer bubbles. If your child is at the Pre-K level, (s)he will most likely have to point to the answer choice. (Answer choices are indicated with corresponding letters in the Answer Key.)

Time: Allow one minute per question, approximately.

Evaluation: The Practice Question Set is labeled by question type. After your child is done, on your own (without your child) go through the Set by question type, writing the number answered correctly in the space provided on the answer key. While these practice questions are not meant to be used in place of an official assessment, these will provide a general overview of strengths/weaknesses, as they pertain to test question type. For questions your child didn't answer correctly, go over the question and answer choices again with him/her. Compare the answer choices, specifically what makes the correct answer choice the right choice.

Since gifted programs typically accept only top performers, you may wish to do additional practice.

Visit **www.GatewayGifted.com** now for test prep coupons, plus a FREE 40-question eBook!

1

○   ○   ○

 2

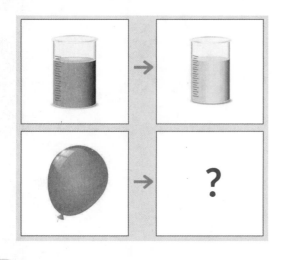

○   ○   ○

 3

○   ○   ○

4

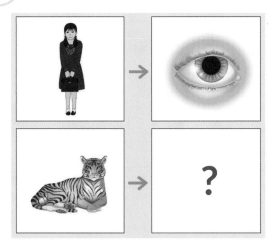 →

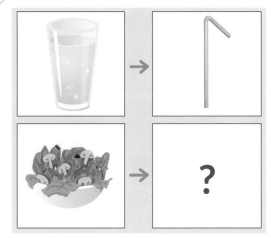 → **?**

○   ○   ○

 5

→

→ **?**

   ○   ○   ○

 6

→

→ **?**

○   ○   ○

7.

○   ○   ○

 8.

   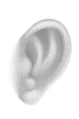

○   ○   ○

 9.

○   ○   ○

10.

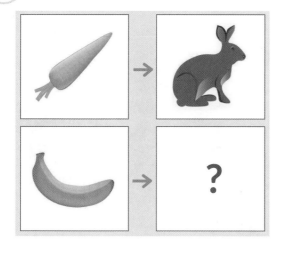

○　　　　　　　　○　　　　　　　　○

 11.

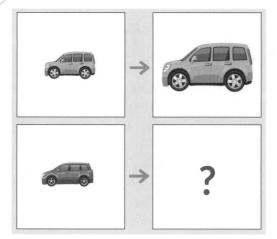

○　　　　　　　　○　　　　　　　　○

12.

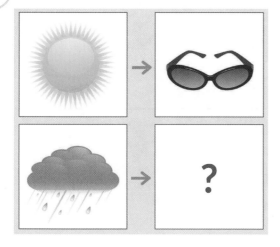

○　　　　　　　　○　　　　　　　　○

13.

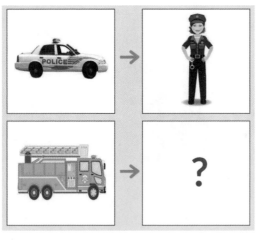

○ ○ ○

14.

○ ○ ○

15.

○ ○ ○

16.

○ ○ ○

 17.

○ ○ ○

 18.

○ ○ ○

19.

○ ○ ○

 20.

○ ○ ○

 21.

○ ○ ○

22.

○ ○ ○

 23.

○ ○ ○

 24.

○ ○ ○

25.

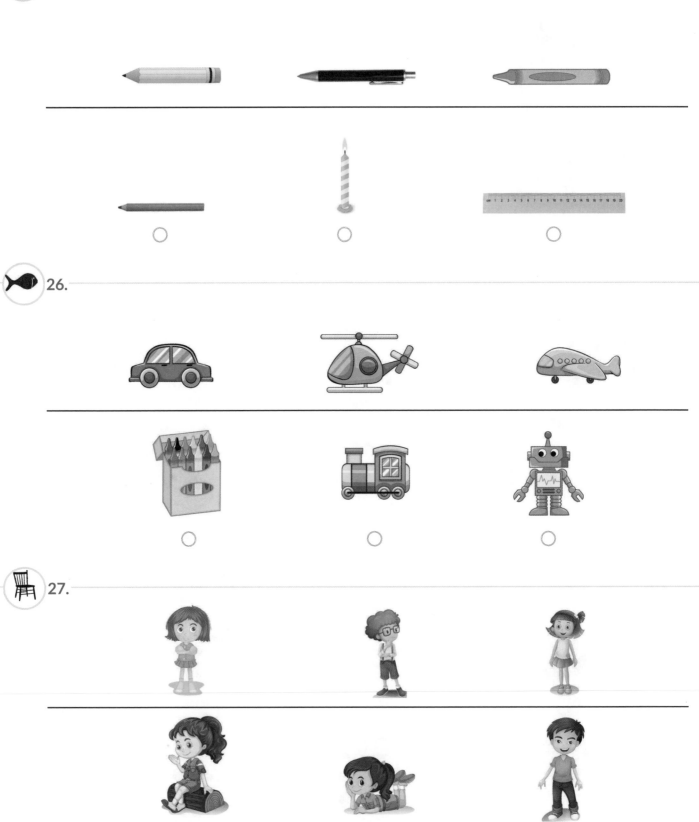

28.

◯ ◯ ◯

 29.

◯ ◯ ◯

 30.

◯ ◯ ◯

31.

○   ○   ○

 32.

○   ○   ○

 33.

○   ○   ○

34.

○   ○   ○

 35.

○   ○   ○

 36.

○   ○   ○

37.

 38.

 39.

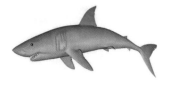

40.

○ ○ ○

End of verbal exercises in Practice Question Set. Continue to the next page.

41.

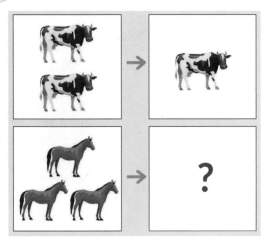

○　　　　　　○　　　　　　○

 42.

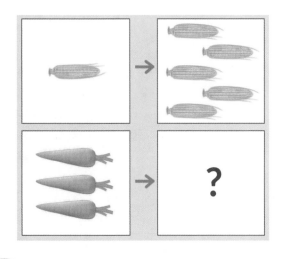

○　　　　　　○　　　　　　○

 43.

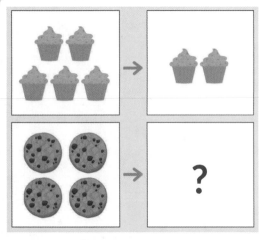

○　　　　　　○　　　　　　○

44.

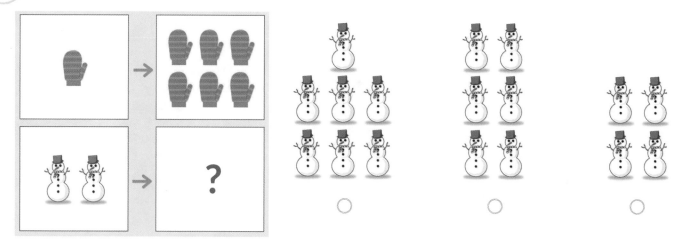

 45.

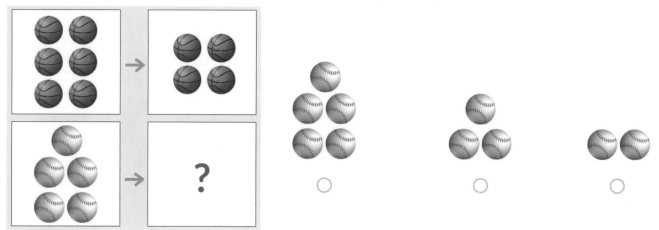

 46.

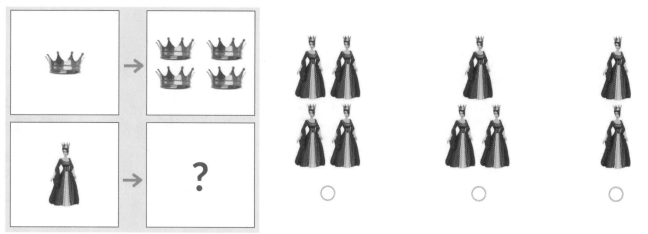

47.

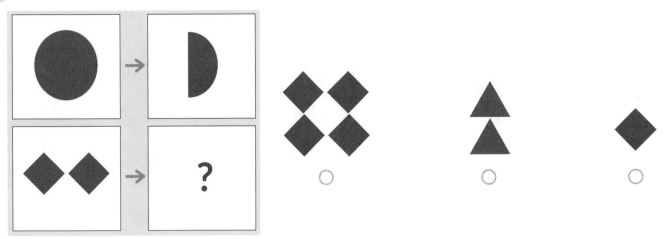

 48.

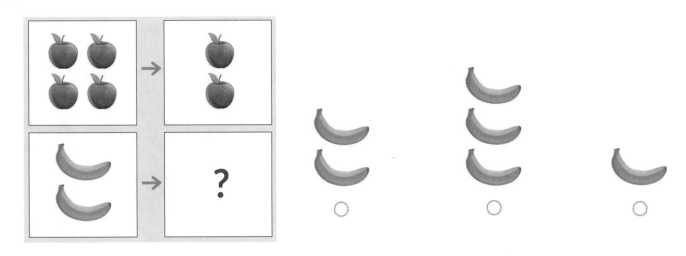

 49.

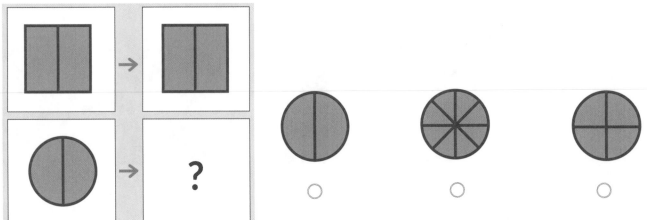

50.

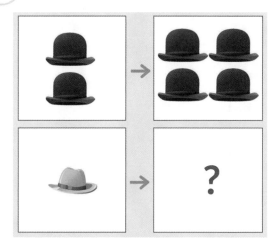

○ ○ ○

 51.

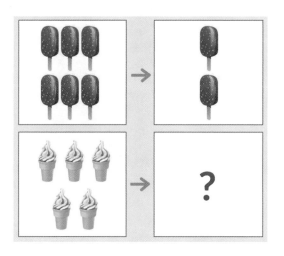

○ ○ ○

Continue to the next page.

52.

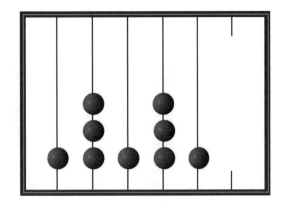 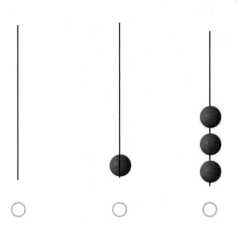

 53.

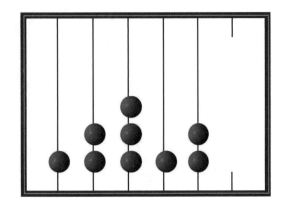 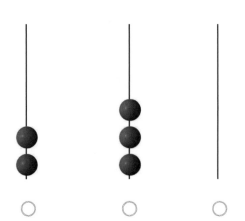

 54.

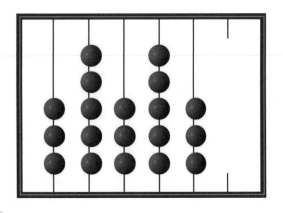 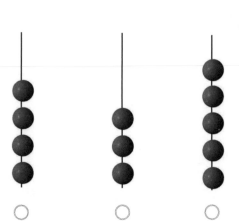

55.

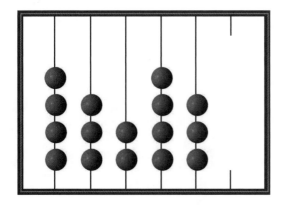

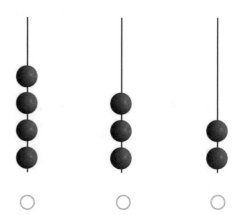

 56.

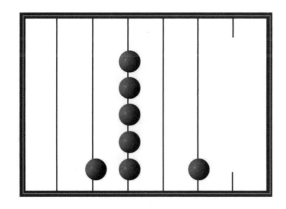

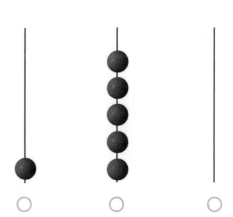

 57.

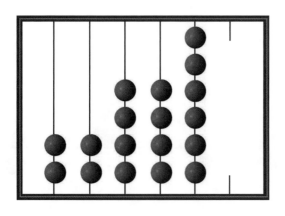

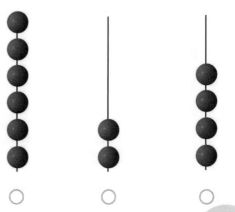

58.

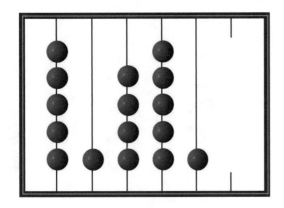

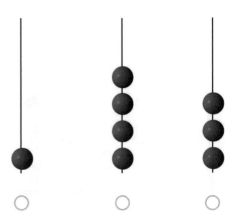

 59.

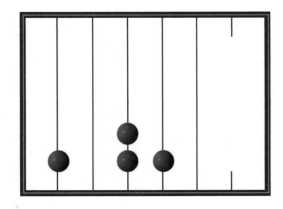

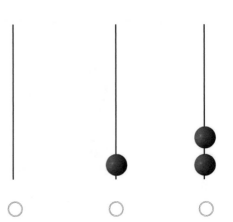

 60.

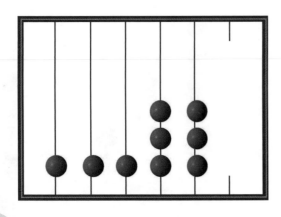

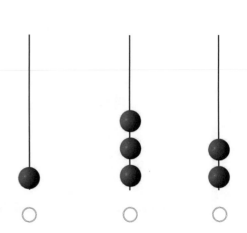

61.

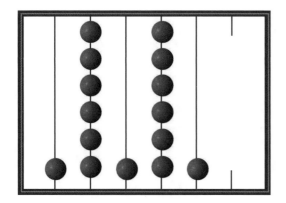

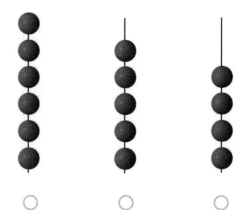

○　　　○　　　○

 62.

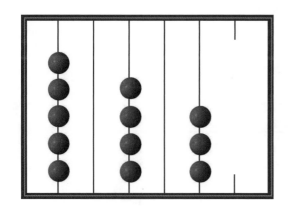

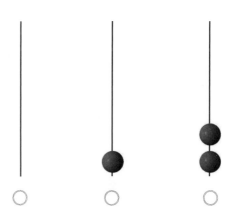

○　　　○　　　○

 63.

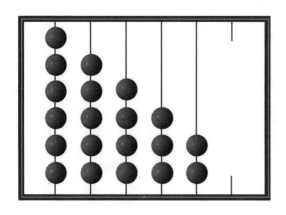

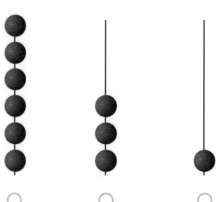

○　　　○　　　○

64.

○ ○ ○

 65.

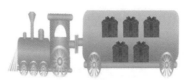

○ ○ ○

 66.

○ ○ ○

67.

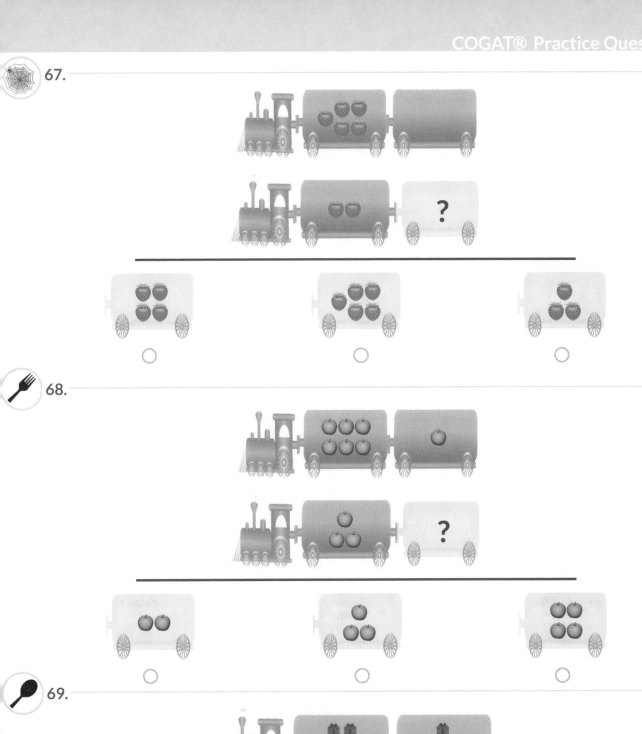

68.

69.

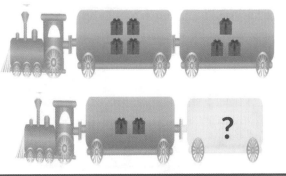

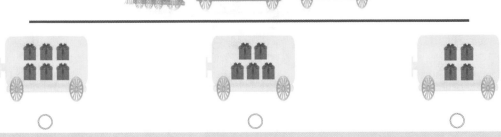

70.

○

○

○

 71.

○

○

○

 72.

○

○

○

73.

○

○

○

74.

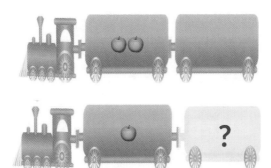

○

○

○

75.

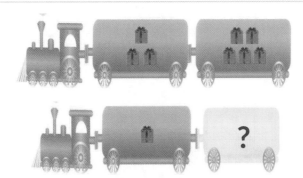

○

○

○

76.

○ ○ ○

77.

○ ○ ○

78.

○ ○ ○

End of quantitative exercises in Practice Question Set. Continue to the next page.

79.

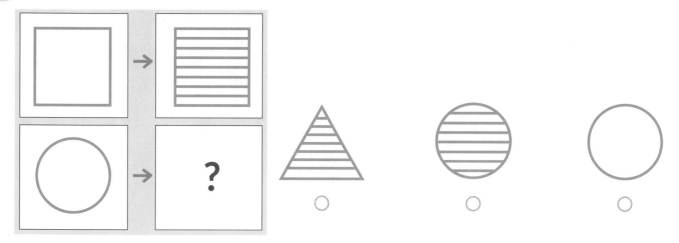

 80.

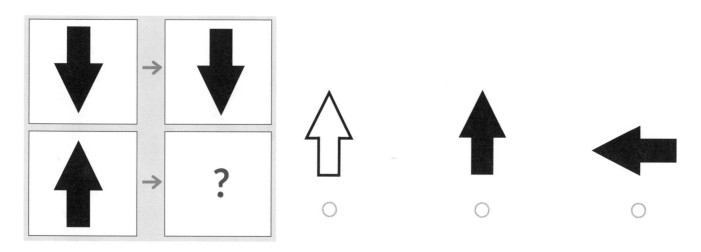

 81.

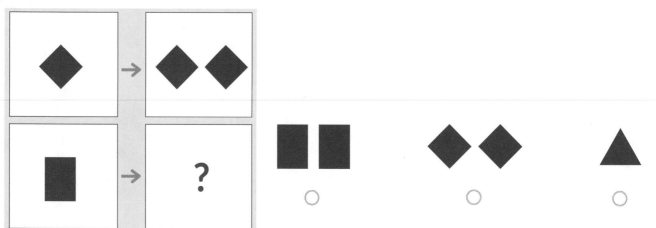

82.

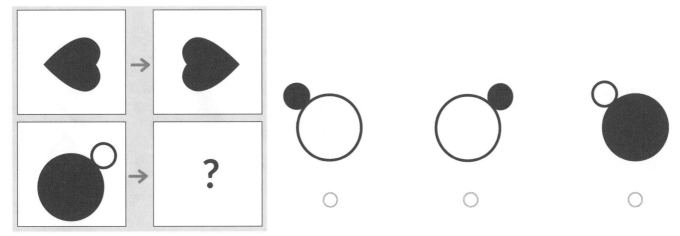

83.

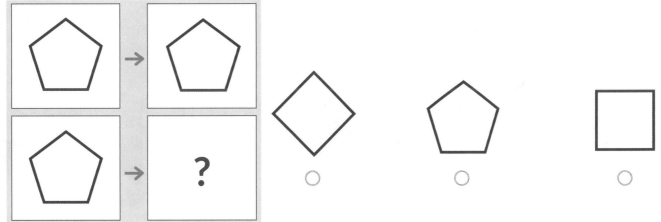

84.

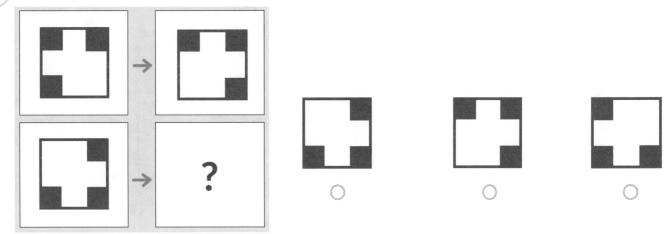

85.

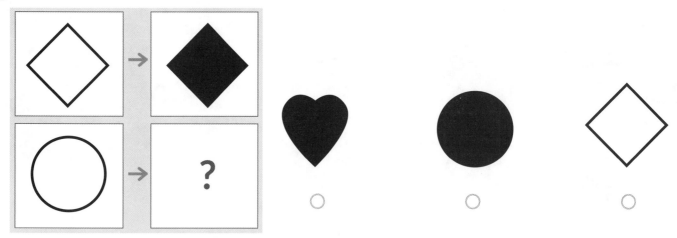

 86.

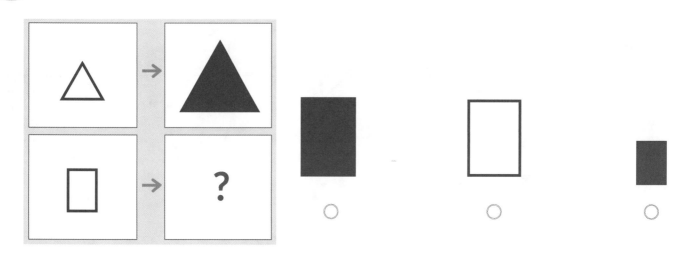

 87.

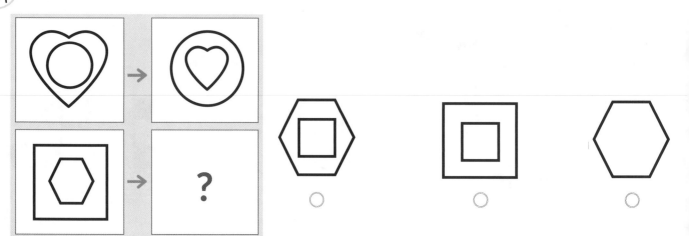

88.

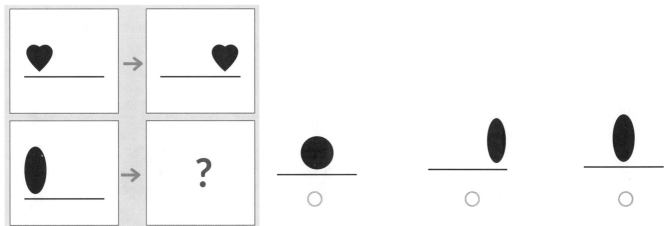

 89.

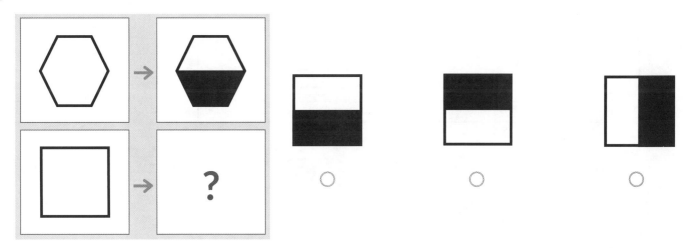

 90.

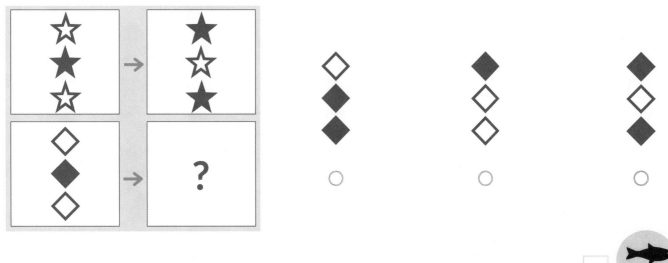

91.

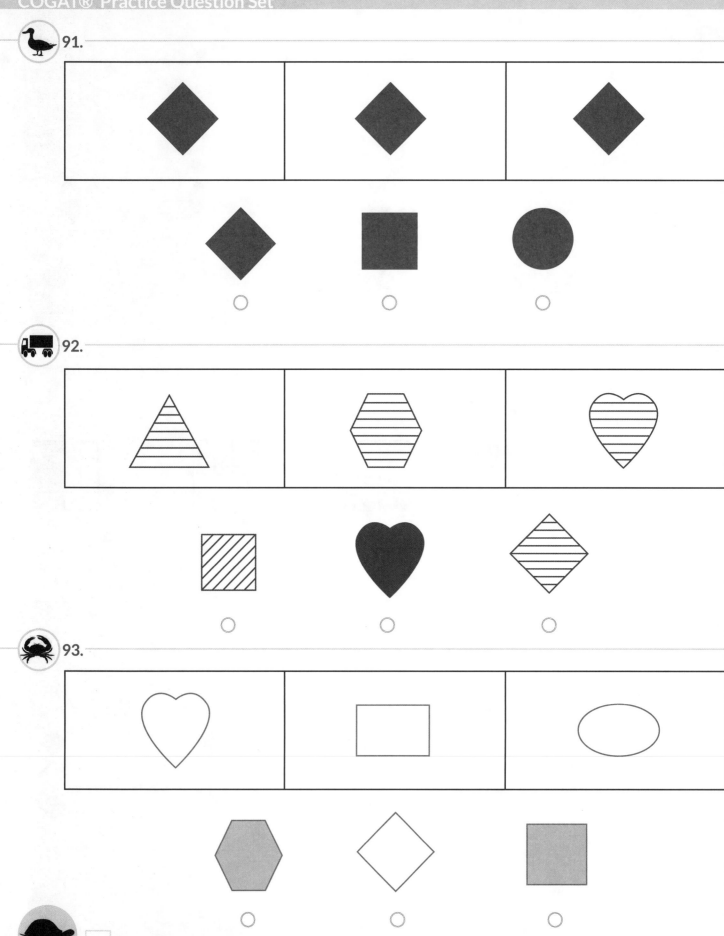

94.

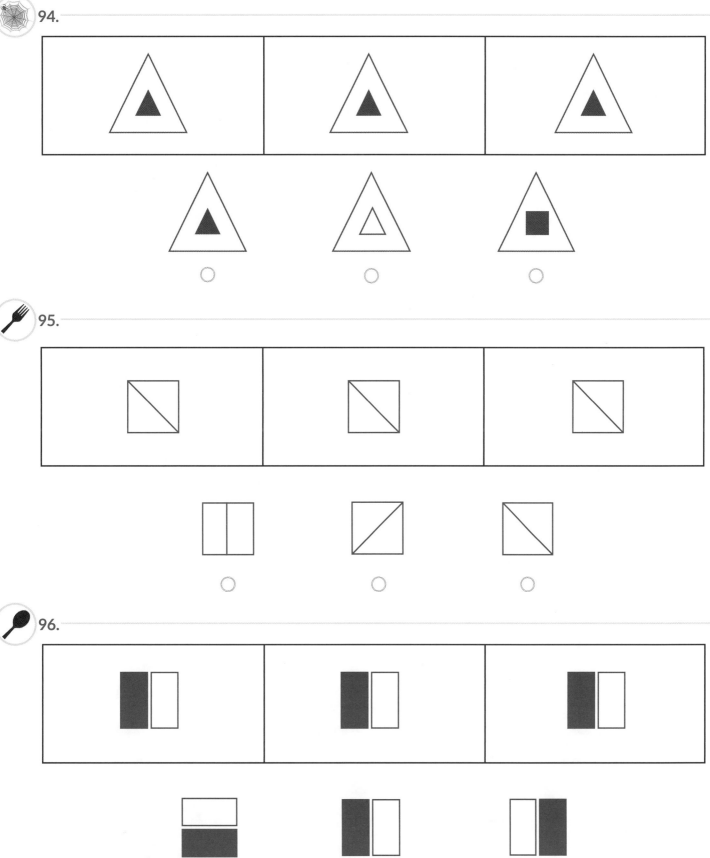

95.

96.

97.

98.

99.

100.

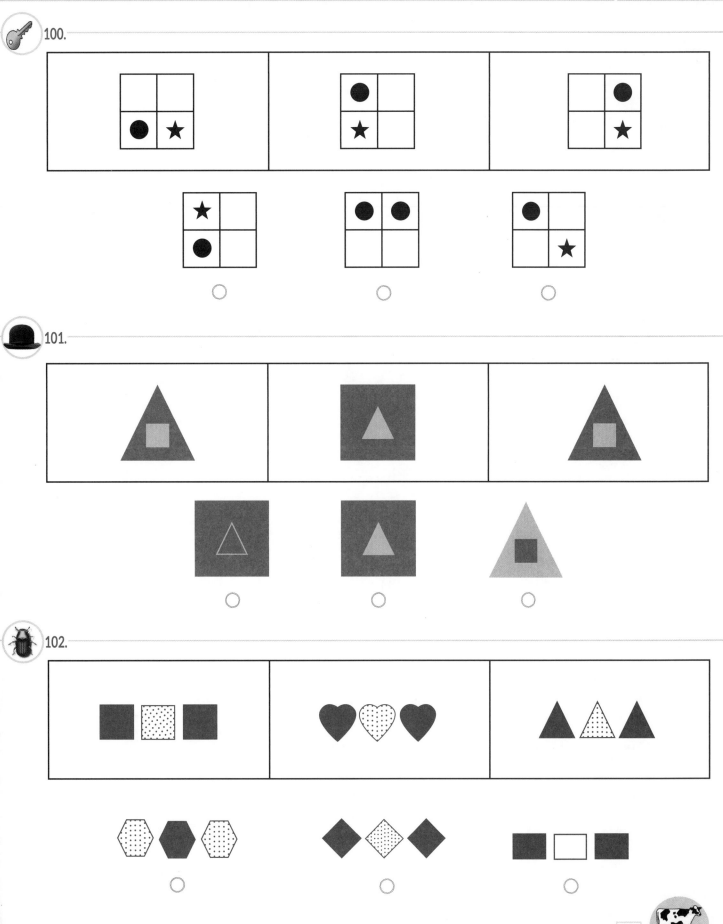

101.

102.

103.

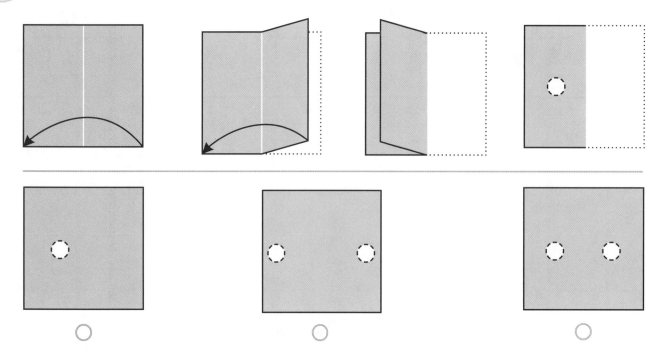

 104.

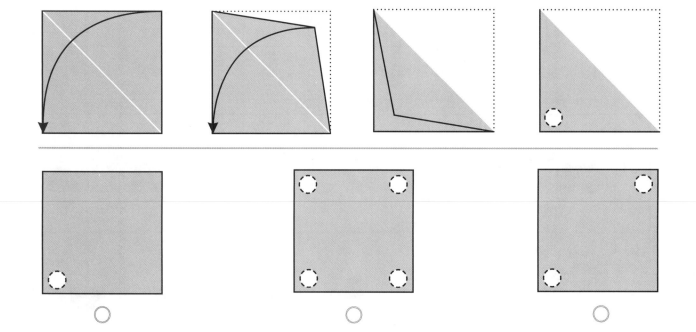

105.

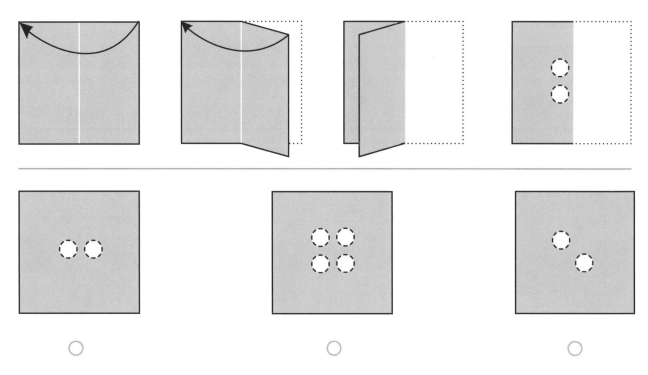

106.

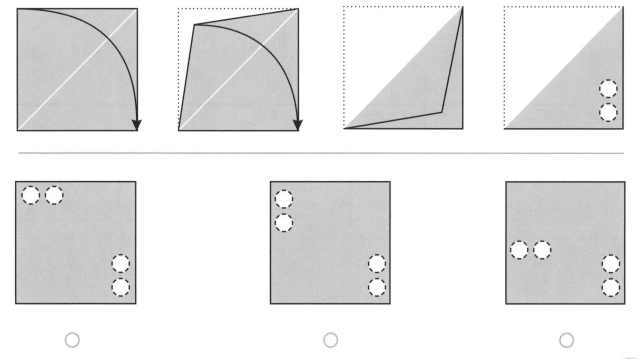

107.

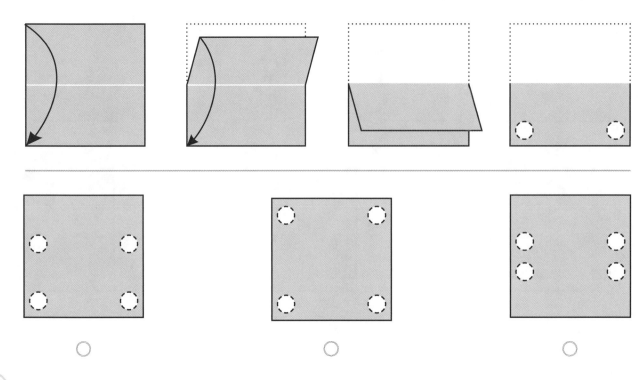

108.

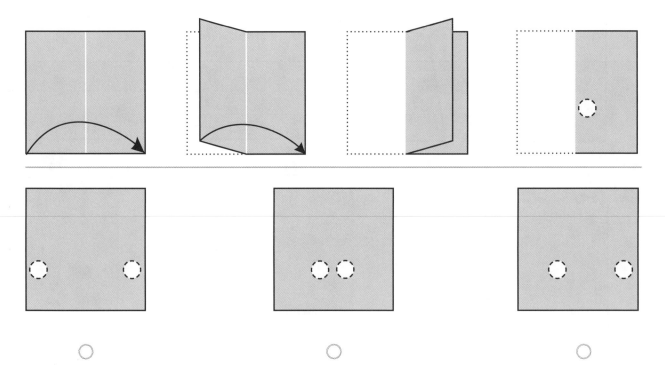

109.

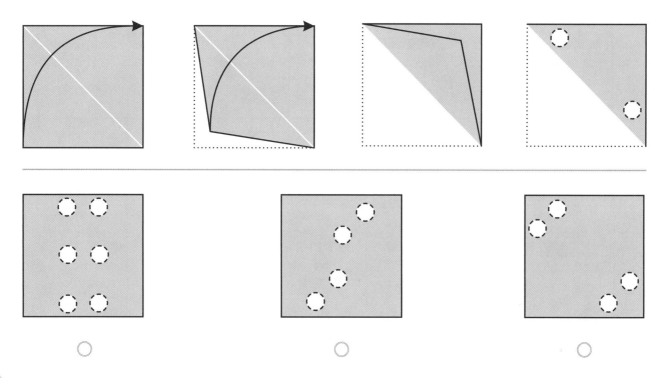

 110.

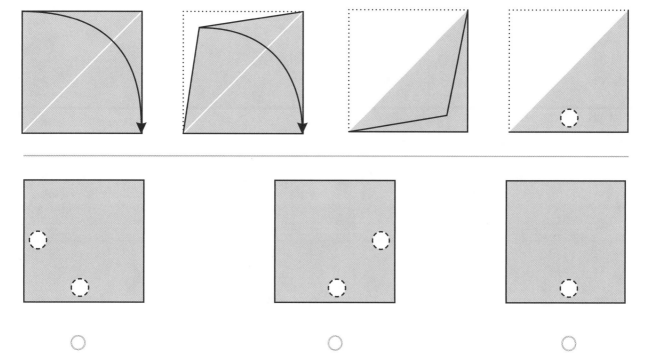

111.

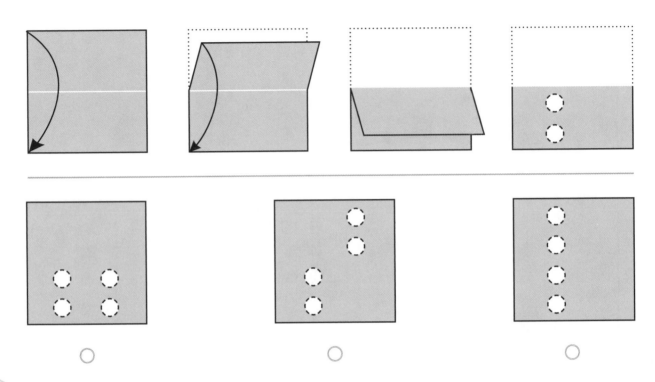

○ ○ ○

 112.

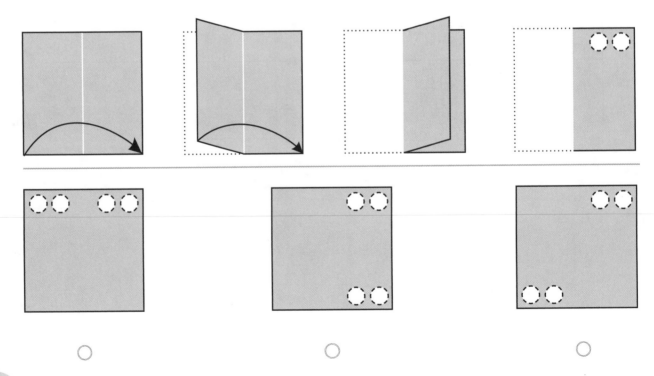

○ ○ ○

ANSWER KEY FOR WORKBOOK (p.10-48)

Identifying Similarities and Differences
1. Items that belong: chocolate, lollipop, cookie, popsicle
2. Shapes that belong: (shapes with vertical lines) oval, hexagon

Identifying Identical Figures
1. A, C   2. B, C   3. C
4. A, B   5. C   6. C   7. C

Identifying Similarities Using Pictures
1. C   2. C   3. A

Identifying Similarities Using Shapes
1. B   2. C   3. A   4. A

Identifying Differences Using Pictures
1. C   2. D   3. B   4. A   5. D   6. B
7. C   8. D   9. A   10. B   11. C   12. B   13. B

Identifying Differences Using Shapes
1. B   2. C   3. B   4. C   5. D   6. B   7. C   8. B

Picture Analogies
1. B   2. B   3. A   4. A   5. C   6. B
7. C   8. A   9. A

Figure Analogies
1. C   2. B   3. C   4. A   5. B   6. C

Picture Classification
1. A   2. B   3. C   4. C   5. A   6. C
7. B   8. C   9. B

Figure Classification
1. C   2. B   3. B   4. A   5. C   6. C

Can You Find It? (Sentence Completion)
1. A   2. B   3. C   4. B   5. A

Paper Folding Puzzles
1. C   2. C   3. A   4. C   5. C   6. B
7. C   8. B

Number Series (Abacus Activity)
1. A   2. B   3. B   4. C   5. A   6. B   7. A

Number Puzzles (Train Activity)
1. B   2. B   3. A   4. A   5. C   6. A   7. C

Number Analogies
1. A   2. C   3. B   4. C   5. B   6. A   7. C

COGAT® PRACTICE QUESTION SET: DIRECTIONS & ANSWER KEY

-Be sure to read 'Practice Question Set Instructions' first (page 49).
-This answer key is divided into charts according to COGAT® question type so that you can easily see how your child performs on each of the test's nine question types. Each chart includes the directions you will read to your child. It also lists the page navigation icons and question navigation icons that you will read to your child to assist with navigation.
1) If turning to a new page, say to your child: "Find the page where there is a(n) ___ at the bottom." (These sentences are listed in each chart in *italics*.)
2) Next, say to your child: "Find the row where there is a(n) ___. " (These are the question navigation icons listed in the first column. They are <u>underlined</u>.)
3) Then, read the directions to your child. These are in the gray box. Each question type has the same directions for the questions of that question type. (The directions are the same for all questions of the same question type.) The only exception is the Sentence Completion questions on p. 92. In the Sentence Completion chart, the directions are in the chart's third column and not in a gray box.

COGAT® QUESTION TYPE 1: PICTURE ANALOGIES

Directions for all Picture Analogy questions: Look at these boxes that are on top. The pictures that are inside belong together in some way. Then, look at these boxes that are on the bottom. One of these boxes on the bottom is empty. Look next to the boxes. There is a row of pictures. Which one would go together with this picture that is in the bottom box like these pictures that are in the top boxes?

"Find the row where there is a(n) _____."	Question Number	Answer	Child's Answer
(p. 50) *"Find the page where there is an umbrella at the bottom."* (Help child find the page where questions start.)			
<u>Shirt</u>	1	A	
<u>Fish</u>	2	B	
<u>Chair</u>	3	A	

continued on the next page

COGAT® QUESTION TYPE 1: PICTURE ANALOGIES, CONTINUED

"Find the row where there is a(n) _____."	Question Number	Answer	Child's Answer
(p. 51) *"Find the page where there is a pair of glasses at the bottom."*			
Car	4	A	
Spiderweb	5	A	
Truck	6	C	
(p. 52) *"Find the page where there is a bird at the bottom."*			
Star	7	B	
Triangle	8	B	
Crab	9	C	
(p. 53) *"Find the page where there is a ball at the bottom."*			
Cup	10	B	
Fork	11	A	
Spoon	12	C	
(p. 54) *"Find the page where there is a train at the bottom."*			
Triangle	13	A	
Cup	14	C	

Picture Analogy Questions Answered Correctly: _____ out of 14

COGAT® QUESTION TYPE 2: PICTURE CLASSIFICATION

Directions for all Picture Classification questions: Look at the top row of pictures. These pictures are alike in a certain way. Then, look at the pictures that are on the bottom row. Which picture that is in the bottom row would go best with the pictures that are in the top row?

"Find the row where there is a(n) _____."	Question Number	Answer	Child's Answer
Heart	15	C	
(p. 55) *"Find the page where there is a house at the bottom."*			
Stoplight	16	A	
Tree	17	C	
Key	18	A	
(p. 56) *"Find the page where there is a triangle at the bottom."*			
Boat	19	B	
Bug	20	B	
Chair	21	A	
(p. 57) *"Find the page where there is a boot at the bottom."*			
Arrow	22	B	
Hat	23	A	
Truck	24	C	
(p. 58) *"Find the page where there is a bug at the bottom."*			
Shirt	25	A	
Fish	26	B	
Chair	27	C	

Picture Classification Questions Answered Correctly: _____ out of 13

COGAT® QUESTION TYPE 3: SENTENCE COMPLETION

"Find the row where there is a(n)___."	Question Number	Directions (Say to child)	Answer	Child's Answer
(p. 59) *"Find the page where there is a key at the bottom."*				
Car	28	Which one of these would you find on a farm?	A	
Spiderweb	29	Which one of these would float in the water?	B	
Shoe	30	Which one of these would a doctor have?	C	
(p. 60) *"Find the page where there is ice cream at the bottom."*				
Bird	31	Which one of these makes things hot?	C	

COGAT® QUESTION TYPE 3: SENTENCE COMPLETION, CONTINUED

Truck	32	Which one of these would a baby chick belong to?	A
Crab	33	Which one of these would you not see in a school?	B

(p. 61) "Find the page where there is a leaf at the bottom."

Spiderweb	34	Which one of these would measure something?	C
Fork	35	Which one of these would swim in water?	C
Bike	36	Which one of these would you not see in the sky?	B

(p. 62) "Find the page where there is a black rectangle at the bottom."

Spoon	37	Which one of these lives in water?	C
Cup	38	Which one of these can fly?	C
Chair	39	Which animal has claws?	B

(p. 63) "Find the page where there is a duck at the bottom."

Star	40	Which one of these would you not see in a bathroom?	C

Sentence Completion Questions Answered Correctly: _____ out of 13

COGAT® QUESTION TYPE 4: NUMBER ANALOGIES

Directions for all Number Analogy questions: Look at these boxes that are on top. The pictures that are inside belong together in some way. Then, look at these boxes that are on the bottom. One of these boxes on the bottom is empty. Look next to the boxes. There is a row of pictures. Which one would go together with this picture that is in the bottom box like these pictures that are in the top boxes?

"Find the row where there is a(n) _____."	Question Number	Answer	Child's Answer
(p. 64) "Find the page where there is a butterfly at the bottom."			
Bike	41	C	
Triangle	42	A	
Crab	43	C	
(p. 65) "Find the page where there is a flower at the bottom."			
Car	44	A	
Fork	45	B	
Spoon	46	A	
(p. 66) "Find the page where there is a black arrow at the bottom."			
Star	47	C	
Bug	48	C	
Crab	49	A	
(p. 67) "Find the page where there is a shirt at the bottom."			
Cup	50	A	
Fork	51	C	

Number Analogies Questions Answered Correctly: _____ out of 11

COGAT® QUESTION TYPE 5: NUMBER SERIES (ABACUS)

Directions for all Number Series questions: Here's an abacus. The "circles" on the abacus are beads. These beads are on rods. The beads on the first five rods have made a pattern. Look at the last rod on the abacus. The beads on this rod are missing. Next to the abacus are three rods. These are the answer choices. Choose which rod would go in the place of the last rod in order to complete the pattern.

"Find the row where there is a(n) _____."	Question Number	Answer	Child's Answer
(p. 68) "Find the page where there is an eye at the bottom."			
Triangle	52	C	
Cup	53	B	
Chair	54	C	
(p. 69) "Find the page where there is a bike at the bottom."			
Stoplight	55	C	
Boat	56	B	
Arrow	57	A	

(p. 70) *"Find the page where there is a fish at the bottom."*

Cup	58	B
Triangle	59	C
Heart	60	B

(p. 71) *"Find the page where there is a spoon at the bottom."*

Key	61	A
Hat	62	A
Bug	63	C

Number Series Questions Answered Correctly: _____ out of 12

COGAT® QUESTION TYPE 6: MATH PUZZLES (TRAIN)

Directions: Look at the trains on the top and bottom. They have things inside. These two trains must have the same number of things. You need to put a train car in place of the train car that has a question mark so that the second train has the same number of things as the other train. Which train car should you choose so that the second train has the same number of things as the first train?

"Find the row where there is a(n) _____."	Question Number	Answer	Child's Answer
(p. 72) *"Find the page where there is a table at the bottom."*			
Pencil	64	C	
Star	65	C	
Crab	66	A	
(p. 73) *"Find the page where there is a hand at the bottom."*			
Spiderweb	67	C	
Fork	68	C	
Spoon	69	B	
(p. 74) *"Find the page where there is a crab at the bottom."*			
Shirt	70	B	
Fish	71	A	
Chair	72	C	
(p. 75) *"Find the page where there is a fork at the bottom."*			
Car	73	A	
Spiderweb	74	C	
Truck	75	C	
(p. 76) *"Find the page where there is a cup at the bottom."*			
Pencil	76	A	
Star	77	C	
Heart	78	C	

Math Puzzles Questions Answered Correctly: _____ out of 15

COGAT® QUESTION TYPE 7: FIGURE ANALOGIES

Directions: Look at these boxes that are on top. The pictures that are inside belong together in some way. Then, look at these boxes that are on the bottom. One of these boxes on the bottom is empty. Look next to the boxes. There is a row of pictures. Which one would go together with this picture that is in the bottom box like these pictures that are in the top boxes?

"Find the row where there is a(n) _____."	Question Number	Answer	Child's Answer
(p. 78) *"Find the page where there is a bug at the bottom."*			
Star	79	B	
Stoplight	80	B	
Crab	81	A	
(p. 79) *"Find the page where there is a hat at the bottom."*			
Cup	82	C	
Fork	83	B	
Spoon	84	C	

COGAT® QUESTION TYPE 7: FIGURE ANALOGIES, CONTINUED

(p. 80) *"Find the page where there is a wheel at the bottom."*

<u>Train</u>	85	B
<u>Cup</u>	86	A
<u>Chair</u>	87	A

(p. 81) *"Find the page where there is a fish at the bottom."*

<u>Stoplight</u>	88	B
<u>Boat</u>	89	A
<u>House</u>	90	C

Figure Analogy Questions Answered Correctly: _____ out of 12

COGAT® QUESTION TYPE 8: FIGURE CLASSIFICATION

Directions: Look at the top row of pictures. The pictures are alike in some way. Then, look at the pictures on the bottom row. Which picture that is in the bottom row would go best with the pictures that are in the top row?

"Find the row where there is a(n) _____."	Question Number	Answer	Child's Answer
(p. 82) *"Find the page where there is a turtle at the bottom."*			
<u>Duck</u>	91	A	
<u>Truck</u>	92	C	
<u>Crab</u>	93	B	
(p. 83) *"Find the page where there is a happy face at the bottom."*			
<u>Spiderweb</u>	94	A	
<u>Fork</u>	95	C	
<u>Spoon</u>	96	B	
(p. 84) *"Find the page where there is a plane at the bottom."*			
<u>Cup</u>	97	B	
<u>Fish</u>	98	A	
<u>Boat</u>	99	B	
(p. 85) *"Find the page where there is a cow at the bottom."*			
<u>Key</u>	100	A	
<u>Hat</u>	101	B	
<u>Bug</u>	102	B	

Figure Classification Questions Answered Correctly: _____ out of 12

COGAT® QUESTION TYPE 9: PAPER FOLDING

Directions: Look at the top row of pictures. These show a sheet of paper, how it was folded, and how holes were made in the folded sheet of paper. Look at these pictures on the bottom row. Which picture shows how the paper would look after it is unfolded?

"Find the row where there is a(n) _____."	Question Number	Answer	Child's Answer
(p. 86) *"Find the page where there is a horse at the bottom."*			
<u>Car</u>	103	C	
<u>Chair</u>	104	C	
(p. 87) *"Find the page where there is a tree at the bottom."*			
<u>Fish</u>	105	B	
<u>Shirt</u>	106	A	
(p. 88) *"Find the page where there is a stoplight at the bottom."*			
<u>Heart</u>	107	B	
<u>Pencil</u>	108	B	
(p. 89) *"Find the page where there is a boat at the bottom."*			
<u>Spiderweb</u>	109	C	
<u>Truck</u>	110	A	
(p. 90) *"Find the page where there is a heart at the bottom."*			
<u>Triangle</u>	111	C	
<u>Key</u>	112	A	

Paper Folding Questions Answered Correctly: _____ out of 10